Friendship

A Book of Quotations

EDITED BY

HERB GALEWITZ

DOVER PUBLICATIONS, INC.
Mineola, New York

DOVER THRIFT EDITIONS

General Editor: Paul Negri
Editor of This Volume: Herb Galewitz

Bibliographical Note

Friendship: A Book of Quotations is a new work, first published by Dover Publications, Inc., in 1999.

Library of Congress Cataloging-in-Publication Data

Friendship : a book of quotations / edited by Herb Galewitz.
 p. cm. — (Dover thrift editions)
 ISBN 0-486-40892-2 (pbk.)
 1. Friendship Quotations, maxims, etc. I. Galewitz, Herb. II. Series.
PN6084.F8F579 1999
177'.62—dc21 99-29903
 CIP

Manufactured in the United States of America
Dover Publications, Inc., 31 East 2nd Street, Mineola, N.Y. 11501

Note

Dictionaries generally define "friend" as one with whom one enjoys mutual affection and regard, "friendship," the relationship between friends. What relatively bland, innocuous definitions for words that inspire so much passion in the pages that follow. Friendship is a concept always in flux, with as many interpretations as individuals who count its blessings and disappointments. So it is not unreasonable to add that friendship seen in this light can be quite a controversial subject—with a preponderance of proponents and many detractors as well. In addition to the negative and positive musings it inspires, friendship in a myriad of forms may also be discerned here. Not only friendship in the most general sense, but woman-woman, woman-man, summer friendships (characterized by "fair-weather friends")—even animal-human friendships—are singled out for special approbation or scorn or both, again, depending upon the particular point of view.

Contradictory sentiments emanating from the same individual may at first glance appear odd or inexplicable, but are easily explained away by the ever-changing nature of human experience; or by the fact that many of these quotations derive from a context in their original source which most readers can only guess at, but lose nothing of the ring of truth in being brought here in a more distilled form.

As this collection amply demonstrates, great minds often seem to differ radically when meditating upon friendship. But not always. For example, it is safe to say in the spirit of the consensus, that money and power are at least obstacles if not downright enemies to friendship; that

no friendship can be called true unless first tried by adversity; and that no one should trust a reconciled friend. And, once in a while, not only do these cogitators agree in concept, they actually converge in splendid detail; to wit:

Walpole (1717–97): If one of my friends happens to die, I drive down to St. James Coffee House, and bring home a new one.

Byron (1788–1824): Let no man grumble when his friends fall off,
As they will do like leaves at the first breeze:
When your affairs come round, one way or t'other,
Go to the coffee-house, and take another.

A friend in power is a friend lost.

One friend in a lifetime is much; two are many; three hardly possible.

Friendship needs a certain parallelism of life, a community of thought, a rivalry of aim.

HENRY ADAMS

Talking with a friend is nothing else but thinking aloud.

Friendship improves happiness, and abates misery, by doubling our joy, and dividing our grief.

> The friendships of the world are oft
> Confederacies in vice, or leagues of pleasure;
> Ours has severest virtue for its basis,
> And such a friendship ends not but with life.
>
> Great souls by instinct to each other turn,
> Demand alliance, and in friendship burn.

JOSEPH ADDISON

A friend who is very near and dear may in time become as useless as a relative.

GEORGE ADE

"Stay" is a charming word in a friend's vocabulary.

BRONSON ALCOTT

A true friend is one soul in two bodies.

In poverty and other misfortunes of life, true friends are a sure refuge. The young they keep out of mischief; to the old they are a comfort and aid in their weakness; and those in the prime of life they incite to noble deeds.

<div align="right">ARISTOTLE</div>

Business, you know, may bring money, but friendship hardly ever does.

Friendship is the finest balm for the pangs of despised love.

<div align="right">JANE AUSTEN</div>

Cosmus, duke of Florence, was wont to say of perfidious friends: 'That we read that we ought to forgive our enemies; but we do not read that we ought to forgive our friends.'

A man cannot speak to his son but as a father, to his wife but as a husband, to his enemy but upon terms; whereas a friend may speak as the case requires, and not as it sorteth with the person.

You may take sarza to open the liver; steel to open the spleen; flowers of sulphur for the lungs; castoreum for the brain; but no receipt openeth the heart but a true friend, to whom you may impart griefs, joys, fears, hopes, suspicions, counsels, and whatsoever lieth upon the heart to oppress it, in a kind of civil shrift or confession.

The best preservative to keep the mind on health is the faithful admonition of a friend.

The worst solitude is to be destitute of sincere friendship.

There is little friendship in the world, and least of all between equals.

Those that want friends to open themselves unto are cannibals of their own hearts.

FRANCIS BACON

Nothing so fortifies a friendship as a belief on the part of one friend that he is superior to the other.

HONORÉ DE BALZAC

No friend is a friend till he shall prove a friend.

BEAUMONT & FLETCHER

Having said, from our respective points of view, the worst thing we can say about each other, having uttered the ultimate insult, there's no reason we can't be friends.

S. N. BEHRMAN

It is well, when one is judging a friend, to remember that he is judging you with the same godlike and superior impartiality.

ARNOLD BENNETT

To live happily with other people one should ask of them only what they can give.

TRISTAN BERNARD

Greater love hath no man than this, that a man lay down his life for his friends.

THE BIBLE (NEW TESTAMENT)

A faithful friend is the medicine of life.

A faithful friend is a strong defense: and he that hath found such an one hath found a treasure.

A friend loveth at all times, and a brother is born for adversity.

Forsake not an old friend, for the new is not comparable to him. A new friend is as new wine: when it is old, thou shalt drink it with pleasure.

Iron sharpeneth iron; so a man sharpeneth the countenance of his friend.

Faithful are the wounds of a friend.

Wealth maketh many friends.

THE BIBLE (OLD TESTAMENT)

Friendship: A ship big enough to carry two in fair weather, but only one in foul.

Acquaintance: A degree of friendship called slight when its object is poor and obscure, and intimate when he is rich and famous.

While your friend holds you affectionately by both your hands, you are safe, for you can watch both his.

AMBROSE BIERCE

Friendship is a word, the very sight of which in print makes the heart warm.

AUGUSTINE BIRRELL

Our friends see the best in us, and by that very fact call forth the best from us.

<div align="right">JOHN BLACK</div>

> The poor make no new friends:—
> But, oh! they love the better still
> The few our Father sends.

<div align="right">HELEN SELINA BLACKWOOD (LADY DUFFERIN)</div>

> Friendship! mysterious cement of the soul!
> Sweet'ner of life, and solder of society!

<div align="right">ROBERT BLAIR</div>

The bird a nest, the spider a web, man friendship.

> Thy friendship oft has made my heart to ache:
> Do be my enemy—for friendship's sake.

> I was angry with my friend
> I told my wrath, my wrath did end.
> I was angry with my foe:
> I told it not, my wrath did grow.

<div align="right">WILLIAM BLAKE</div>

Friends are like fiddle-strings, they must not be screwed too tight.

Few there are that will endure a true friend.

He that ceaseth to be a friend never was a good one.

<div align="right">H. G. BOHN</div>

Kindred weaknesses induce friendships as often as kindred virtues.

False friends are like our shadow, keeping close to us as we walk in the sunshine, but leaving us the instant we cross into the shade.

<div align="right">CHRISTIAN NESTELL BOVEE</div>

<div align="center">Hand</div>
Grasps at hand, eye lights eye in good friendship,
And great hearts expand
And grow one in the sense of this world's life.

<div align="right">ROBERT BROWNING</div>

Friendship is the only cure for hatred, the only guarantee of peace.

<div align="right">GAUTAMA BUDDHA</div>

There is no man so friendless but what he can find a friend sincere enough to tell him disagreeable truths.

Whatever the number of a man's friends, there will be times in his life when he has too few.

<div align="right">EDWARD GEORGE BULWER-LYTTON</div>

I would rather have five energetic and competent enemies than one fool friend.

<div align="right">LUTHER BURBANK</div>

Love comes from blindness, friendship from knowledge.

<div align="right">COMTE DE BUSSY-RABUTIN</div>

A friend who cannot at a pinch remember a thing or two that never happened is as bad as one who does not know how to forget.

Friendship is like money, easier made than kept.

A man's friendships are, like his will, invalidated by marriage — but they are no less invalidated by the marriage of his friends.

The dead being the majority, it is natural that we should have more friends among them than among the living.

SAMUEL BUTLER

I have found that a friend may profess, yet deceive.

Friendship is Love without his wings!

> Let no man grumble when his friends fall off,
> As they will do like leaves at the first breeze:
> When your affairs come round, one way or t'other,
> Go to the coffee-house, and take another.
>
> But the poor dog, in life the firmest friend,
> The first to welcome, foremost to defend.

LORD BYRON (GEORGE GORDON)

> Give me the avowed, erect and manly foe;
> Firm I can meet, perhaps return the blow;
> But of all plagues, good Heaven, thy wrath can send,
> Save, save, oh! save me, from the candid friend.

GEORGE CANNING

Do you want to make friends? Be friendly. Forget yourself.

<div align="right">DALE CARNEGIE</div>

Friendship, in the old heroic sense of that term, no longer exists; . . . it is in reality no longer expected or recognized as a virtue among men.

<div align="right">THOMAS CARLYLE</div>

Treasure that gadfly, that friend who shows you your faults.

<div align="right">FRANK CASE</div>

Only solitary men know the full joys of friendship. Others have their family; but to a solitary and an exile his friends are everything.

<div align="right">WILLA CATHER</div>

Friendship's a noble name, 'tis love refined.

<div align="right">SUSANNAH CENTLIVRE</div>

Women give nothing to friendship except what they borrow from love.

<div align="right">SÉBASTIEN CHAMFORT</div>

Trust not a reconciled friend, for good turns cannot blot out old grudges.

Flatterers look like friends, as wolves like dogs.

<div align="right">GEORGE CHAPMAN</div>

Friends through fortune become enemies through mishap.

GEOFFREY CHAUCER

A woman can become a man's friend only in the following stages—first an acquaintance, next a mistress, and only then a friend.

ANTON CHEKHOV

Most people enjoy the inferiority of their best friends.

LORD CHESTERFIELD

There are a good many fools who call me a friend, and also a good many friends who call me a fool.

G. K. CHESTERTON

Every murderer is probably somebody's old friend.

AGATHA CHRISTIE

Greatly his foes he dreads, but more his friends; he hurts me most who lavishly commends.

WINSTON CHURCHILL

Love is the attempt to form a friendship inspired by beauty.

You must . . . love me, myself, and not my circumstances, if we are to be real friends.

A friend is, as it were, a second self.

Friendship makes prosperity brighter, while it lightens adversity by sharing its griefs and anxieties.

<div align="right">CICERO</div>

A woman's friendship borders more closely on love than man's. Men affect each other in the reflection of noble or friendly acts; whilst women ask fewer proofs and more signs and expressions of attachment.

> Alas! they had been friends in youth;
> But whispering tongues can poison truth.
>
> Flowers are lovely; Love is flower-like;
> Friendship is a sheltering tree.
>
> Old friends burn dim, like lamps in noisome air;
> Love them for what they are; nor love them less,
> Because to thee they are not what they were.

<div align="right">SAMUEL TAYLOR COLERIDGE</div>

To accept a favour from a friend is to confer one.

<div align="right">JOHN CHURTON COLLINS</div>

Friendship often ends in love; but love in friendship—never.

Our very best friends have a tincture of jealousy even in their friendship; and when they hear us praised by others, will ascribe it to sinister and interested motives if they can.

If you want enemies, excel others; if you want friends, let others excel you.

<div align="right">CHARLES CALEB COLTON</div>

There are three friendships which are advantageous, and three which are injurious. Friendship with the upright; friendship with the sincere; and friendship with the man of much observation; these are advantages. Friendship with the man of specious airs; friendship with the insinuatingly soft; and friendship with the glib-tongued; these are injurious.

Between friends, frequent reproofs make the friendship distant.

Have no friends not equal to yourself.

<div align="right">CONFUCIUS</div>

You shall judge of a man by his foes as well as by his friends.

<div align="right">JOSEPH CONRAD</div>

The man that hails you Tom or Jack,
And proves by thumping on your back
 How he esteems your merit,
Is such a friend, that one had need
Be very much his friend indeed
 To pardon or to bear it.

How sweet, how passing sweet, is solitude!
But grant me still a friend in my retreat,
Whom I may whisper, Solitude is sweet.

I would not enter on my list of friends,
(Though grac'd with polish'd manners and fine sense,
Yet wanting sensibility) the man
Who needlessly sets foot upon a worm.

<div align="right">WILLIAM COWPER</div>

What is a Friend? I will tell you. It is a person with whom you dare to be yourself.

<div align="right">FRANK CRANE</div>

Good fellowship is common, but unchanging affection is not.

<div align="right">CLARENCE DAY</div>

The best way to keep your friends is to never borrow from them and never lend them anything.

<div align="right">PAUL DE KOCK</div>

Chance makes our parents, but choice makes our friends.

<div align="right">JACQUES DELILLE</div>

Friends are as dangerous as enemies.

<div align="right">THOMAS DE QUINCEY</div>

Friends—those relations that one makes for one's self.

<div align="right">EUSTACHE DESCHAMPS</div>

A friend to all is a friend to none.

When Zeno was asked what a friend was, he replied, "Another I."

<div align="right">DIOGENES LÄERTIUS</div>

Generally speaking, among sensible persons, it would seem that a rich man deems that friend a sincere one who does not want to borrow his money; while, among the less favored with fortune's gifts, the sincere friend is generally esteemed to be the individual who is ready to lend it.

A female friend, amiable, clever, and devoted, is a possession more valuable than parks and palaces; and without such a muse, few men can succeed in life, none be contented.

BENJAMIN DISRAELI

Friends are ourselves.

JOHN DONNE

To find a friend one must close one eye—to keep him, two.

NORMAN DOUGLAS

For friendship, of itself a holy tie,
Is made more sacred by adversity.

The wretched have no friends.

JOHN DRYDEN

There are no friends at cards or world politics.

FINLEY PETER DUNNE

Friendships which are born in misfortune are more firm and lasting than those which are formed in happiness.

THOMAS D'URFEY

So, if I live or die to serve my friend,
'Tis for my love—'tis for my friend alone,
And not for any rate that friendship bears
In heaven or on earth.

Best friend, my well-spring in the wilderness!

Friendship should be more than biting Time can sever.

Friendships begin with liking or gratitude—roots that can be pulled up.

Animals are such agreeable friends. They ask no questions, they pass no criticisms.

<div align="right">George Eliot</div>

We want but two or three friends, but these we cannot do without, and they serve us in every thought we think.

A man's growth is seen in the successive choirs of his friends.

A friend is a person with whom I may be sincere. Before him, I may think aloud.

Better be a nettle in the side of your friend than his echo.

The condition which high friendship demands is ability to do without it.

A friend may well be reckoned the masterpiece of nature.

Friends are fictions founded on some single momentary experience.

Friends, such as we desire, are dreams and fables.

Friendship, like the immortality of the soul, is too good to be believed.

Happy is the house that shelters a friend.

I do then with my friends as I do with my books. I would have them where I could find them, but I seldom use them.

The only way to have a friend is to be one.

Oh, be my friend, and teach me to be thine!

The only reward of virtue is virtue; the only way to have a friend is to be one.

I hate the prostitution of the name of friendship to signify modish and worldly alliances.

We take care of our health, we lay up money, we make our roof tight and our clothing sufficient, but who provides wisely that he shall not be wanting in the best property of all—friends?

Friendship should be surrounded with ceremonies and respects, and not crushed into corners. Friendship requires more time than poor, busy men can usually command.

It is sublime to feel and say of another, I need never meet, or speak, or write to him; we need not reinforce ourselves or send tokens of remembrance; I rely on him as on myself; if he did thus or thus, I know it was right.

> A day for toil, an hour for sport,
> But for a friend is life too short.

<div align="right">RALPH WALDO EMERSON</div>

In prosperity it is very easy to find a friend; in adversity, nothing is so difficult.

When our friends are present we ought to treat them well; and when they are absent, to speak of them well.

<div align="right">EPICTETUS</div>

When ill befalls, a friend's kind eye beams comfort.

Life has no blessing like a prudent friend.

EURIPIDES

Promises may get friends, but it is performance that must nurse and keep them.

OWEN FELTHAM

It is in the thirties that we want friends. In the forties we know they won't save us any more than love did.

F. SCOTT FITZGERALD

A woman-friend! He that believes that weakness steers in a stormy night without a compass.

JOHN FLETCHER

Old dog Tray's ever faithful;
 Grief can not drive him away;
He is gentle, he is kind—
 I'll never, never find
A better friend than old dog Tray!

STEPHEN COLLINS FOSTER

A false Friend and a Shadow attend only while the Sun shines.

A brother may not be a friend, but a friend will always be a brother.

There are three faithful friends—an old wife, an old dog, and ready money.

Be slow in choosing a friend, slower in changing.

<div align="right">BENJAMIN FRANKLIN</div>

The beauty of enmity is insecurity; the beauty of friendship is in security.

<div align="right">ROBERT FROST</div>

A reconciled Friend is a double Enemy.

Even reckonings keep long friends.

All are not friends that speak us fair.

He's a friend that speaks well on's behind our backs.

Be a friend to thyself and others will be so too.

Friendship that flames goes out in a flash.

He is my friend that succoreth me, not he that pitieth me.

If you have one true friend you have more than your share.

May it please God not to make our friends so happy as to forget us!

Nature teaches us to love our friends, but religion our enemies.

No man can be happy without a friend, nor be sure of his friend till he is unhappy.

Make not a bosom friend of a melancholy soul: he'll be sure to aggravate thy adversity, and lessen thy prosperity. He goes away heavy loaded: and thou must bear half.

A broken friendship may be solder'd, but will never be sound.

THOMAS FULLER

"What is the secret of your life?" asked Mrs. Browning of Charles Kingsley. "Tell me, that I may make mine beautiful, too." He replied: "I had a friend."

RELATED BY WILLIAM CHANNING GARRETT

A woman's friendship ever ends in love.

From wine that sudden friendships spring.

> Friendship, like love, is but a name.
> An open foe may prove a curse,
> But a pretended friend is worse.
>
> 'Tis thus that on the choice of friends
> Our good or evil name depends.
>
> Who friendship with a knave hath made,
> Is judg'd a partner in the trade.

JOHN GAY

True friendship comes when silence between two people is comfortable.

DAVE TYSON GENTRY

Friendship is always a sweet responsibility, never an opportunity.

KAHLIL GIBRAN

What good is a friend if you can't make an enemy of him?

<div align="right">WILLIAM GILLETTE</div>

It is better to be deceived by one's friends than to deceive them.

Liking and even love contribute nothing to friendship.

<div align="right">GOETHE</div>

And what is friendship but a name,
 A charm that lulls to sleep:
A shade that follows wealth or fame,
 But leaves the wretch to weep?

Friendship is a disinterested commerce between equals; love, an abject intercourse between tyrants and slaves.

Friendships that are disproportioned ever terminate in disgust.

He cast off his friends, as a huntsman his pack;
For he knew, when he pleased, he could whistle them back.

<div align="right">OLIVER GOLDSMITH</div>

Friends are a second existence.

A wise man gets more use from his enemies than a fool from his friends.

<div align="right">BALTASAR GRACIÁN</div>

A favourite has no friend!

<div align="right">THOMAS GRAY (ON A FAVOURITE CAT DROWNED)</div>

A friend is one with whom we are fond of being when no business is afoot nor any entertainment contemplated.

Better to trust an open enemy than a reconciled friend.

ROBERT GREENE

Friendship cannot live with ceremony, nor without civility.

It is a misfortune for a man not to have a friend in the world, but for that reason he shall have no enemy.

LORD HALIFAX

He who has made the acquisition of a judicious and sympathetic friend, may be said to have doubled his mental resources.

ROBERT HALL

Green be the turf above thee,
 Friend of my better days!
None knew thee but to love thee,
 Nor named thee but to praise.

FITZ-GREENE HALLECK

I have no trouble with my enemies. But my Goddam friends, . . . they are the ones that keep me walking the floors nights.

WARREN G. HARDING

We never know the true value of friends. While they live we are too sensitive of their faults: when we have lost them we only see their virtues.

Friendship closes its eye, rather than see the moon eclipst; while malice denies that it is ever at the full.

Friendship is Love, without either flowers or veil.

<div align="right">J. C. AND A. W. HARE</div>

Contracting a real friendship is one of the most completely involuntary things a man can do.

<div align="right">HENRY S. HASKINS</div>

The dupe of friendship, and the fool of love; have I not reason to hate and to despise myself? Indeed I do; and chiefly for not having hated and despised the world enough.

He will never have true friends who is afraid of making enemies.

Discussing the character and foibles of common friends is a great sweetener and cement of friendship.

Even in the common affairs of life, in love, friendship, and marriage, how little security have we when we trust our happiness in the hands of others!

<div align="right">WILLIAM HAZLITT</div>

It is a mark of friendship to imagine the worst possible things about a friend.

<div align="right">BEN HECHT</div>

My friends and gnats together have gone with the sunny weather.

<div align="right">HEINRICH HEINE</div>

Our friendship was so assured that we could be silent without the slightest danger of offence.

<div align="right">SIR ARTHUR HELPS</div>

The best mirror is an old friend.

Before you make a friend eat a bushel of salt with him.

It is good to have some friends both in Heaven and Hell.

<div align="right">GEORGE HERBERT</div>

Wilt thou my true friend be?
Then love not mine, but me.

<div align="right">ROBERT HERRICK</div>

Sweet is the scene where genial friendship plays
The pleasing game of interchanging praise.

<div align="right">OLIVER WENDELL HOLMES</div>

A generous friendship no cold medium knows,
Burns with one love, with one resentment glows;
One should our interests and our passions be,
My friend must hate the man that injures me.

Praise from a friend, or censure from a foe,
Are lost on hearers that our merits know.

My friend should honor him who honors me.

Two friends, two bodies with one soul inspir'd.

<div align="right">HOMER</div>

Nothing shall I, while sane, compare with a friend.

'Tis hard to find a man of great estate, that can distinguish flatterers from friends.

Wise were the kings who never chose a friend till with full cups they had unmasked his soul, and seen the bottom of his deepest thoughts.

To have a great man for an intimate friend seems pleasant to those who have never tried it; those who have, fear it.

True friends appear less mov'd than counterfeit.

<div align="right">HORACE</div>

Summer friends vanish when the cask is drained to the dregs.

<div align="right">HORATIUS</div>

It was not foes to conquer,
Nor sweethearts to be kind,
But it was friends to die for
That I would seek and find.

<div align="right">A. E. HOUSMAN</div>

Friendship lives on its income, love devours its capital.

<div align="right">ARSENE HOUSSAYE</div>

Probably no man ever had a friend he did not dislike a little; we are all so constituted by nature no one can possibly entirely approve of us.

A man's best friend is seldom his neighbor.

Don't abuse your friends and expect them to consider it criticism.

Instead of loving your enemies, trust your friends a little better.

I don't want my friends to die for me; if they will be polite, and let me alone, I will be satisfied.

<div align="right">E. W. HOWE</div>

Distance sometimes endears friendship and absence sweeteneth it.

Friendship is the great chain of human society.

It is a rule in friendship, when Distrust enters in at the foregate, Love goes out at the postern.

Make not thy friend too cheap to thee, nor thyself too dear to him.

<div align="right">JAMES HOWELL</div>

If you have a friend worth loving,
 Love him. Yes, and let him know
That you love him, ere life's evening
 Tinge his brow with sunset glo.
Why should good words ne'er be said
 Of a friend till he is dead?

<div align="right">DANIEL W. HOYT</div>

Your friend is the man who knows all about you, and still likes you.

Friendship: To do unto someone that which you would not allow him to do unto you.

<div align="right">ELBERT HUBBARD</div>

A friend that ain't in need is a friend indeed.

The fellow that calls you "brother" usually wants something that doesn't belong to him.

<div align="right">KIN HUBBARD</div>

A friend married is a friend lost.

The costliness of keeping friends does not lie in what one does for them, but in what one, out of consideration for them, refrains from doing.

<div align="right">HENRIK IBSEN</div>

Whenever a man's friends begin to compliment him about looking young, he may be sure that they think he is growing old.

> Sweet is the memory of distant friends!
> Like the mellow rays of the departing sun,
> It falls tenderly, yet sadly, on the heart.

<div align="right">WASHINGTON IRVING</div>

The first thing to learn in intercourse with others is non-interference with their own peculiar ways of being happy, provided those ways do not assume to interfere by violence with ours.

<div align="right">WILLIAM JAMES</div>

I find friendship to be like wine, raw when new, ripened with age, the true old man's milk and restorative cordial.

An injured friend is the bitterest of foes.

I find as I grow older that I love those most whom I loved first.

I never considered a difference of opinion in politics, in religion, in philosophy, as cause for withdrawing from a friend.

<div align="right">THOMAS JEFFERSON</div>

Friendship, peculiar boon of Heav'n,
 The noble mind's delight and pride,
To men and angels only giv'n,
 To all the lower world denied.

Friendship, compounded of esteem and love, derives from one its tenderness and its permanence from the other.

Friends are often chosen for similitude of manners, and therefore each palliate the other's failings because they are his own.

If a man does not make new acquaintance as he advances through life, he will soon find himself left alone. A man . . . should keep his friendship in constant repair.

Always . . . set a high value on spontaneous kindness. He whose inclination prompts him to cultivate your friendship of his own accord, will love you more than one whom you have been at pains to attach to you.

I love the acquaintance of young people; because in the first place, I don't like to think myself growing old. In the next place, young acquaintances must last longest, if they do last; and then young men have more virtue than old men; they have more generous sentiments in every respect.

The enduring elegance of female friendship.

It is as foolish to make experiments upon that constancy of a friend, as upon the chastity of a wife.

Most friendships are formed by caprice or by chance—mere confederacies in vice or leagues in folly.

The great effect of friendship is beneficence, yet by the first act of uncommon kindness it is endangered.

The longer we live, and the more we think, the higher value we learn to put on the friendship and tenderness of parents and friends. Parents we can have but once; and he promises himself too much, who enters life with the expectation of finding many friends.

The most fatal disease of friendship is gradual decay, or dislike hourly increased by causes too slender for complaint, and too numerous for removal.

A friend may be often found and lost, but an old friend never can be found, and nature has provided that he cannot easily be lost.

SAMUEL JOHNSON

True happiness
Consists not in the multitude of friends,
But in the worth and choice. Nor would I have
Virtue a popular regard pursue:
Let them be good that love me, though but few.

BEN JONSON

Friendship is too pure a pleasure for a mind cankered with ambition or the lust of power and grandeur.

The fortune that made you a king, forbade you to have a friend. It is a law of nature, which cannot be violated with impunity.

<div align="right">JUNIUS</div>

Friendship is the hobby-horse of all the moral rhetoricians; it is nectar and ambrosia to them.

<div align="right">IMMANUEL KANT</div>

'Tis sweet, as year by year we lose
Friends out of sight, in faith to muse
How grows in Paradise our store.

<div align="right">JOHN KEBLE</div>

Love and friendship exclude each other.

One faithful Friend is enough for a man's self; 'tis much to meet with such an one, yet we can't have too many for the sake of others.

Two persons will not be friends long if they cannot forgive each other little failings.

In friendship we see only those faults which may injure our friend; in love we see only those which injure ourselves.

<div align="right">JEAN DE LA BRUYÈRE</div>

A true friend is a pearl. He reads
Your deepest needs
And so spares you the shame
Of giving your heart's hidden desires a name.

Friendship is the shadow of the evening which strengthens with the setting sun of life.

Nothing is more dangerous than a friend without discretion; even a prudent enemy is preferable.

<div align="right">JEAN DE LA FONTAINE</div>

It is good to have friends at court.

<div align="right">CHARLES LAMB</div>

No friendship is so cordial or so delicious as that of girl for girl; no hatred so intense and immovable as that of woman for woman.

Friendship is a vase which, when it is flawed by heat, or violence, or accident, may as well be broken at once; it can never be trusted after.

<div align="right">WILLIAM SAVAGE LANDOR</div>

In friendship, as in love, we are often more happy from the things we are ignorant of than from those we are acquainted with.

The greatest medicine is a true friend.

However rare true love is, true friendship is rarer.

What men have given the fame of friendship to is nothing but an alliance, a reciprocal accommodation of interests, an exchange of good offices; it is a species of commerce out of which self-love always expects to gain something.

When our best friends are in trouble, there is always something that is not wholly displeasing to us.

When we exaggerate the tenderness of our friends towards us, it is often less from gratitude than from a desire to exhibit our own merit.

What causes the majority of women to be so little touched by friendship is that it is insipid when they have once tasted of love.

LA ROCHEFOUCAULD

If you want to make a dangerous man your friend, let him do you a favor.

LEWIS F. LAWES

He is a fine friend. He stabs you in the front.

LEONARD LOUIS LEVINSON

Show me a friend in need and I will show you a pest.

JOE E. LEWIS

I desire so to conduct the affairs of this administration that if at the end, when I come to lay down the reins of power, I have lost every other friend on earth, I shall at least have one friend left, and that friend shall be down inside of me.

ABRAHAM LINCOLN

It is an old belief
 That on some solemn shore,
Beyond the sphere of grief,
 Dear friends shall meet once more.

JOHN GIBSON LOCKHART

Platonic friendship: The interval between the introduction and the first kiss.

SOPHIE IRENE LOEB

O friend! O best of friends! Thy absence more
Than the impending night darks the landscape o'er!

And the song, from beginning to end, I found again in the heart of a friend.

Come back! ye friendships long departed!
That like o'erflowing streamlets started,
And now are dwindled, one by one,
To stony channels in the sun!
Come back! ye friends, whose lives are ended,
Come back, with all that light attended,
Which seemed to darken and decay
When ye arose and went away!

HENRY WADSWORTH LONGFELLOW

There is no friendship between those associated in power; he who rules will always be impatient of an associate.

LUCAN

He who advises you to be reserved to your friends wishes to betray you without witnesses.

MANUEL CONDE LUCANOR

Time draweth wrinkles in a fair face, but addeth fresh colors to a fast friend, which neither heat, nor cold, nor misery, nor place, nor destiny, can alter or diminish.

When adversities flow, then love ebbs; but friendship standeth stiffly in storms.

JOHN LYLY

Women, like princes, find few real friends.

LORD LYTTLETON

A true friend is forever a friend.

As you grow ready for it, somewhere or other you will find what is needful for you in a book or a friend.

Better to have a loving friend than ten admiring foes.

GEORGE MACDONALD

Friendships, like marriages, are dependent on avoiding the unforgivable.

JOHN D. MACDONALD

He who reckons ten friends has not one.

CHRÉTIEN MALESHERBES

The richer your friends, the more they will cost you.

ELIZABETH MARBURY

O summer-friendship,
Whose flattering leaves, that shadowed us in our
Prosperity, with the least gust drop off
In the Autumn of adversity.

PHILIP MASSENGER

The capacity for friendship is God's way of apologizing for our families.

JAY MCINERNEY

A man of active and resilient mind outwears his friendships just as certainly as he outwears his love affairs, his politics and his epistemology.

H. L. MENCKEN

In a dissension between a man and a wife, that one is in the right who has the most friends.

GEORGE MEREDITH

Friends are like melons. Shall I tell you why?
To find one good, you must a hundred try.

CLAUDE MERMET

The golden period, when I had not a single friend.

HENRY MILLER

A good friend will do almost anything for you except read the books you insist upon lending him.

MILWAUKEE JOURNAL

The best way to keep your friends is not to give them away.

The man who won't loan money isn't going to have many friends—or need them.

WILSON MIZNER

He who is the friend of all humanity is not my friend.

I like to be distinguished; and to cut the matter short, the friend of all mankind is no friend of mine.

The more we love our friends, the less we flatter them; it is by excusing nothing that pure love shows itself.

<div align="right">MOLIÈRE</div>

Admonitions and corrections are the chief duties of friendship.

Friends and friendship are nothing but acquaintanceships and familiarities formed by some chance or convenience.

Friendship is a creature formed for a companionship, not for a herd.

Friendship, unlike love, which is weakened by fruition, grows up, thrives, and increases by enjoyment; and being of itself spiritual, the soul is reformed by the habit of it.

<div align="right">MONTAIGNE</div>

Friendship is an arrangement by which we undertake to exchange small favors for big ones.

<div align="right">BARON DE MONTESQUIEU</div>

There is no stronger bond of friendship than a mutual enemy.

<div align="right">FRANKFORT MOORE</div>

Oh, call it by some better name,
For Friendship sounds too cold.

Shall I give up the friend I have
 valued and tried,
If he kneel not before the same altar
 with me?

The thread of our life would be dark,
 Heaven knows!
If it were not with friendship and love
 intertwined.

<div align="right">THOMAS MOORE</div>

A friend in deeds is a friend indeed.

God gives us our relatives; thank God we can choose our friends.

It is better to make friends fast than to make fast friends.

<div align="right">ETHEL WATTS MUMFORD</div>

He treats his enemies as if they might someday become his friends, and his friends as if they might become his enemies.

<div align="right">NAPOLEON</div>

Companionship is a matter of mutual weaknesses. We like that man or woman best who has the same faults we have.

Love demands infinitely less than friendship.

<div align="right">GEORGE JEAN NATHAN</div>

A home-made friend wears longer than one you buy in the market.

<div align="right">AUSTIN O'MALLEY</div>

But oh! if grief thy steps attend,
 If want, if sickness be thy lot,
And thou require a soothing friend,
 Forget me not, forget me not!

<div align="right">AMELIA OPIE</div>

In the life of a young man the most essential thing for happiness is the gift of friendship.

<div align="right">SIR WILLIAM OSLER</div>

As the yellow gold is tried in fire, so the faith of friendship must be seen in adversity.

The vulgar herd estimate friends by the advantage to be derived from them.

<div align="right">OVID</div>

A girl's best friend is her mutter.

<div align="right">DOROTHY PARKER</div>

If all men knew what each said of the other, there would not be four friends in the world.

<div align="right">BLAISE PASCAL</div>

The friendship between me and you I will not compare to a chain; for that the rains might rust, or the falling tree might break.

A true friend unbosoms freely, advises justly, assists readily, adventures boldly, takes all patiently, defends courageously, and continues a friend unchangeably.

There can be no friendship where there is no freedom. Friendship loves a free air, and will not be fenced up in straight and narrow enclosures.

WILLIAM PENN

You can always tell a real friend: when you've made a fool of yourself he doesn't feel you've done a permanent job.

LAURENCE J. PETER

True friendship between man and man is infinite and immortal.

PLATO

Prosperity makes friends and adversity tries them.

Nothing is there more friendly to a man than a friend in need.

PLAUTUS

A constant friend is a thing rare and hard to find.

The flatterer's object is to please in everything he does; whereas the true friend always does what is right, and so often gives pleasure, often pain, not wishing the latter, but not shunning it either, if he deems it best.

PLUTARCH

Absent or dead, still let a friend be dear.

Trust not yourself; but your defects to know,
Make use of ev'ry friend—and ev'ry foe.

There is nothing that is meritorious but virtue and friendship; and, indeed, friendship itself is only a part of virtue.

How often are we to die before we go quite off this stage? In every friend we lose a part of ourselves, and the best part.

> I know the thing that's most uncommon;
> (Envy, be silent and attend!)
> I know a reasonable woman,
> Handsome and witty, yet a friend.

Histories are more full of examples of the fidelity of dogs than of friends.

<div align="right">ALEXANDER POPE</div>

A friend is one who dislikes the same people that you dislike.

A friend that you buy, will be bought from you.

A true friend should be like a privy, open in necessity.

Love is blind; friendship closes its eyes.

It is good to have friends, but bad to need them.

Friends help; others pity.

You can hardly make a friend in a year, but you can easily lose one in an hour.

A good friend is better than a near relation.

They are not all friends who laugh with you.

Friends are lost by calling often and calling seldom.

It is worse to mistrust a friend than to be deceived by him.

When we go up the hill of fortune may we never meet a man coming down.

Be a friend to thyself, and others will be so too.

Choose thy friends like thy books, few but choice.

Friends are like fiddle-strings, they must not be screwed too tight.

If you have one true friend, you have more than your share.

Friends are thieves of time.

A friend in need is a friend indeed.

A friend is never known till a man have need.

A friend in court is better than a penny in purse.

Time, which strengthens friendship, weakens love.

A lost friendship is an enmity won.

Friendship is love with understanding.

Friendship made in a moment is of no moment.

Speak well of your friend, of your enemy say nothing.

The friends of my friends are my friends.

The enemy of my enemy is my friend.

Trust not a new friend nor an old enemy.

Save a man from his friends, and leave him to struggle with his enemies.

Wealth maketh many friends.

Friendship is a prodigal, but love is a miser.

When I lend I am a friend, when I ask I am a foe.

Happy is he whose friends were born before him.

Everyman's friend is everyman's fool.

Beware of the friend who was once your foe.

Sudden friendship, sure repentance.

No friendship can survive the gift of gold.

PROVERBS

That friendship will not continue to the end which is begun for an end.

FRANCIS QUARLES

If thy friends be of better quality than thyself, thou mayest be sure of two things; the first, they will be more careful to keep thy counsel, because they have more to lose than thou hast; the second, they will esteem thee for thyself, and not for that which thou dost possess.

SIR WALTER RALEIGH

Friendship among women is only a suspension of hostilities.

ANTOINE DE RIVAROL

Friends—people who borrow books and set wet glasses on them.

<div align="right">EDWIN ARLINGTON ROBINSON</div>

In life our absent friend is far away:
But death may bring our friend exceeding near.

<div align="right">CHRISTINA ROSSETTI</div>

Was it a friend or foe that spread these lies?
Nay, who but infants question in such wise,
'Twas one of my most intimate enemies.

<div align="right">DANTE GABRIEL ROSSETTI</div>

Friendship is the ideal; friends are the reality; the reality always remains far apart from the ideal.

<div align="right">JOSEPH ROUX</div>

If we were all given by magic the power to read each other's thoughts, I suppose the first effect would be to dissolve all friendships.

<div align="right">BERTRAND RUSSELL</div>

A friend whom you have been gaining during your whole life, you ought not to be displeased with in a moment. A stone is many years becoming a ruby; take care that you do not destroy it in an instant against another stone.

<div align="right">SAADI (SHEIKH MUSLIH ADDIN)</div>

The sacrifices of friendship were beautiful in her eyes as long as she was not asked to make them.

<div align="right">SAKI (H. H. MUNRO)</div>

To desire the same things and to reject the same things, constitutes true friendship.

<div align="right">SALLUST</div>

Friends are generally of the same sex, for when men and women agree, it is only in their conclusions; their reasons are always different.

As widowers proverbially marry again, so a man with the habit of friendship always finds new friends.

One's friends are that part of the human race with which one can be human.

<div align="right">GEORGE SANTAYANA</div>

Every time I paint a portrait I lose a friend.

<div align="right">JOHN SINGER SARGENT</div>

You'll find the friendship of the world mere outward show!— 'Tis like the harlot's tears, the statesman's promise, or the false patriot's zeal, full of fair seeming but delusion all.

<div align="right">RICHARD SAVAGE</div>

My friend shows what I can do, and my foe what I should.

<div align="right">FRIEDRICH VON SCHILLER</div>

Everyone's friend is no one's.

With most people there will be no harm in occasionally mixing a grain of disdain with your treatment of them; that will make them value your friendship all the more.

Friends and acquaintances are the surest passports to fortune.

<div align="right">SCHOPENHAUER</div>

Know this, that he that is a friend of himself is a friend to all men.

Friendship always benefits; love sometimes injures.

<div align="right">SENECA</div>

I am wealthy in my friends.

There is flattery in friendship.

I rather wish you foes than hollow friends.

I will never love that which my friend hates.

Friendship's full of dregs.

A friend should bear his friend's infirmities.

Most friendship is feigning, most loving mere folly.

The band that seems to tie their friendship together will be the very strangler of their amity.

Call you that backing of your friends? A plague upon such backing! give me them that will face me.

> Freeze, freeze, thou bitter sky,
> That does not bite so nigh
> As benefits forgot:
> Though thou the waters warp.
> Thy sting is not so sharp
> As friend remember'd not.

Those friends thou hast, and their adoption tried,
Grapple them to thy soul with hoops of steel,
But do not dull thy palm with entertainment
Of each new hatched, unfledged comrade.

 Those you make friends
And give your hearts to, when they once perceive
The least rub in your fortunes, fall away
Like water from ye, never found again
But where they mean to sink ye.

Words are easy, like the wind;
Faithful friends are hard to find.

Two lovely berries moulded on one stem:
So, with two seeming bodies, but one heart.

What viler thing upon the earth than friends
Who can bring noblest minds to basest ends!

Neither a borrower nor a lender be;
For loan oft loses both itself and friend.

I count myself in nothing else so happy
As in a soul remembering my good friends.

Friendship is constant in all other things
Save in the office and affairs of love.

But if the while I think on thee, dear friend,
All losses are restor'd and sorrows end.

The amity that wisdom knits not, folly
May easily untie.

He that is thy friend indeed,
He will help thee in thy need.

WILLIAM SHAKESPEARE

Have you not heard
When a man marries, dies or turns Hindoo,
His best friends hear no more of him?

To be omnipotent but friendless is to reign.

<div align="right">PERCY BYSSHE SHELLEY</div>

There is no word in the Latin language that signifies a female friend. *Amica* means a mistress: and perhaps there is no friendship betwixt the sexes wholly disunited from a degree of love.

<div align="right">WILLIAM SHENSTONE</div>

Friendship is the bond of reason.

<div align="right">RICHARD BRINSLEY SHERIDAN</div>

Be careful to make friendship the child and not the father of virtue, for many are rather good friends than good men; so, although they do not like the evil their friend does, yet they like him who does the evil; and though no counselors of the offence, they yet protect the offender.

<div align="right">SIR PHILIP SIDNEY</div>

If a man is worth knowing at all, he is worth knowing well.

<div align="right">ALEXANDER SMITH</div>

Hearts that are delicate and kind and tongues that are neither—these make the finest company in the world.

I might give my life for a friend, but he'd better not ask me to do up a parcel.

The mere process of growing old together will make our slightest acquaintances seem like bosom friends.

We need new friends; some of us are cannibals who have eaten their old friends up; others must have ever-renewed audiences before whom to re-enact an ideal version of their lives.

LOGAN PEARSALL SMITH

Madam, I have been looking for a person who disliked gravy all my life; let us swear eternal friendship.

REV. SYDNEY SMITH

Be slow to fall into friendship; but when thou art in continue firm and constant.

Force is of no use to make or preserve a friend, who is an animal that is never caught nor tamed but by kindness and pleasure.

SOCRATES

'Tis something to be willing to commend;
But my best praise is, that I am your friend.

THOMAS SOUTHERNE

A friend is a present you give yourself.

No man is useless while he has a friend.

The truth that is suppressed by friends is the readiest weapon of the enemy.

It's an owercome sooth fo' age an' youth,
 And it brooks wi' nae denial,
That the dearest friends are the auldest friends,
 And the young are just on trial.

<div align="right">ROBERT LOUIS STEVENSON</div>

Friendships are discovered rather than made.

<div align="right">HARRIET BEECHER STOWE</div>

He who betrays a friend, shall never be
Under one roof, or in one ship, with me.

I am weary of friends, and friendships are all monsters.

I have been gaining enemies by the scores, and friends by the couples, which is against the rules of wisdom, because they say one enemy can do more hurt than ten friends can do good.

Two friendships in two breasts requires the same aversions and desires.

Two women seldom grow intimate but at the expense of a third person.

When we are old, our friends find it difficult to please us, and are less concerned whether we be pleased or not.

<div align="right">JONATHAN SWIFT</div>

Stately, kindly, lordly friend,
 Condescend
Here to sit by me.

<div align="right">ALGERNON CHARLES SWINBURNE (*TO A CAT*)</div>

I cannot, having been your lover,
Stoop to become your friend!

ARTHUR SYMONS

Treat your friend as if he might become your enemy.

A friend must not be injured, even in jest.

Unless you bear with the faults of a friend you betray your own.

Reprove your friends in secret, praise them openly.

PUBLILIUS SYRUS

Flattery is natural in friends.

TACITUS

Never speak ill of yourself; your friends will say enough on that subject.

Mme. de Staël is such a good friend, she would throw all her friends into the river for the pleasure of fishing them out.

CHARLES MAURICE DE TALLEYRAND

Ascend a step to choose a friend, descend a step to choose a wife.

THE TALMUD

Friendship's the privilege
Of private men; for wretched greatness knows
No blessing so substantial.

NAHUM TATE

Friendship is the allay of our sorrows, the ease of our passions, the discharge of our oppressions, the sanctuary to our calamities, the counselor of our doubts, the clarity of our minds, the emission of our thoughts, the exercise and improvement of what we meditate.

Friendship is like rivers, and the strand of seas, and the air, common to all the world; but tyrants, and evil customs, wars, and want of love, have made them proper and peculiar.

Some friendships are made by nature, some by contract, some by interest, and some by souls.

Nature and religion are the bands of friendship, excellence and usefulness are its great endearments.

JEREMY TAYLOR

Then came your new friend: you began to change—
I saw it and grieved.

ALFRED LORD TENNYSON

Of my friends, I am the only one I have left.

TERENCE

True friends visit us in prosperity only when invited, but in adversity they come without invitation.

THEOPHRASTUS

Against a foe I can myself defend,—
But Heaven protect me from a blundering friend!

D'ARCY WENTWORTH THOMPSON

A man cannot be said to succeed in this life who does not satisfy one friend.

Friends will be much apart. They will respect more each other's privacy than their communion.

I have three chairs in my house; one for solitude, two for friendship, three for company.

Nothing makes the earth seem so spacious as to have friends at a distance: they make the latitudes and longitudes.

The most I can do for my friend is simply to be his friend. I have no wealth to bestow on him. If he knows that I am happy in loving him, he will want no other reward. Is not friendship divine in this?

What is commonly called friendship is only a little more honor among rogues.

HENRY DAVID THOREAU

In politics . . . shared hatreds are almost always the basis of friendships.

ALEXIS DE TOCQUEVILLE

An infallible way of acquiring a host of friends is to be a host yourself.

One's friends are divided into two classes, those who knows one because one must and those one knows because one mustn't.

SYDNEY TREMAYNE

It takes your enemy and your friend, working together, to hurt you to the heart, the one to slander you and the other to get the news to you.

The holy passion of Friendship is of so sweet and steady and loyal and enduring a nature that it will last through a whole lifetime, if not asked to lend money.

There is always something about your success that displeases even your best friends.

There is an old time toast which is golden for its beauty. 'When you ascend the hill of prosperity, may you not meet a friend.'

MARK TWAIN

Friendship, take heed; if woman interfere,
Be sure the hour of thy Destruction's near.

SIR JOHN VAN BRUGH

God save me from my friends, I can protect myself from my enemies.

MARSHAL DE VILLARS

Friendship is the marriage of the soul.

Our friends abandon us only too easily, and our enemies are implacable.

VOLTAIRE

If one of my friends happens to die, I drive down to St. James Coffee House, and bring home a new one.

HORACE WALPOLE

I love such mirth as does not make friends ashamed to look upon one another the next morning.

IZAAK WALTON

True friendship is a plant of slow growth, and must undergo and withstand the shocks of adversity before it is entitled to the appellation.

A slender acquaintance with the world must convince every man, that actions, not words, are the true criterion of the attachment of friends; and that the most liberal professions of good-will are very far from being the surest marks of it.

GEORGE WASHINGTON

We cherish our friends not for their ability to amuse us, but for ours to amuse them.

EVELYN WAUGH

When you are down and out something always turns up— and it's usually the noses of your friends.

ORSON WELLES

He's the kind of man who picks his friends—to pieces.

MAE WEST

But lasting joys the man attend
Who has a polished female friend.

REV. CORNELIUS WHUR

An acquaintance that begins with a compliment is sure to develop into a real friendship.

Anybody can sympathize with the sufferings of a friend, but it requires a very fine nature to sympathize with a friend's success.

Friendship is more tragic than love. It lasts longer.

Instead of loving your enemies, treat your friends a little better.

Laughter is not at all a bad beginning for a friendship, and it is far the best ending for one.

OSCAR WILDE

The path of social advancement is, and must be, strewn with broken friendships.

H. G. WELLS

Friendship is not possible between two women one of whom is very well dressed.

I have lost friends, some by death . . . others by sheer inability to cross the street.

VIRGINIA WOOLF

Of friends, however humble, scorn not one.

<div align="right">WILLIAM WORDSWORTH</div>

New friends, like new mistresses, are got by disparaging old ones.

<div align="right">WILLIAM WYCHERLEY</div>

Friendship's the wine of life: but friendship new . . . is neither strong nor pure.

<div align="right">EDWARD YOUNG</div>

It is one of the ironies of life that our intimates often provoke us more than our enemies.

<div align="right">EDWARD W. ZIEGLER</div>

DOVER·THRIFT·EDITIONS

All books complete and unabridged. All 5³⁄₁₆" x 8¹⁄₄," paperbound.
Just $1.00–$2.00 in U.S.A.

A selection of the more than 200 titles in the series.

POETRY

AFRICAN-AMERICAN POETRY: An Anthology, 1773–1930, Joan R. Sherman (ed.). 96pp. 29604-0 $1.00

SELECTED POEMS, Paul Laurence Dunbar. 80pp. 29980-5 $1.00

BEST POEMS OF THE BRONTË SISTERS (ed. by Candace Ward), Emily, Anne and Charlotte Brontë. 64pp. 29529-X $1.00

GREAT POEMS BY AMERICAN WOMEN: An Anthology, Susan L. Rattiner (ed.). 224pp. (Available in U.S. only) 40164-2 $2.00

"GOD'S GRANDEUR" AND OTHER POEMS, Gerard Manley Hopkins. 80pp. 28729-7 $1.00

THE CONCORD HYMN AND OTHER POEMS, Ralph Waldo Emerson. 64pp. 29059-X $1.00

DOVER BEACH AND OTHER POEMS, Matthew Arnold. 112pp. 28037-3 $1.50

HARDY'S SELECTED POEMS, Thomas Hardy. 80pp. 28753-X $1.50

BHAGAVADGITA, Bhagavadgita. 112pp. 27782-8 $1.50

SONGS OF INNOCENCE AND SONGS OF EXPERIENCE, William Blake. 64pp. 27051-3 $1.00

BLAKE'S SELECTED POEMS, William Blake. 96pp. 28517-0 $1.00

THE CLASSIC TRADITION OF HAIKU: An Anthology, Faubion Bowers (ed.). 96pp. 29274-6 $1.50

AENEID, Vergil (Publius Vergilius Maro). 256pp. 28749-1 $2.00

SONNETS FROM THE PORTUGUESE AND OTHER POEMS, Elizabeth Barrett Browning. 64pp. 27052-1 $1.00

MY LAST DUCHESS AND OTHER POEMS, Robert Browning. 128pp. 27783-6 $1.00

POEMS AND SONGS, Robert Burns. 96pp. 26863-2 $1.00

SELECTED POEMS, George Gordon, Lord Byron. 112pp. 27784-4 $1.50

SELECTED POEMS FROM "FLOWERS OF EVIL," Charles Baudelaire. 64pp. 28450-6 $1.00

THE RIME OF THE ANCIENT MARINER AND OTHER POEMS, Samuel Taylor Coleridge. 80pp. 27266-4 $1.00

SELECTED POEMS, Emily Dickinson. 64pp. 26466-1 $1.00

SELECTED POEMS, John Donne. 96pp. 27788-7 $1.50

THE RUBÁIYÁT OF OMAR KHAYYÁM: FIRST AND FIFTH EDITIONS, Edward FitzGerald. 64pp. 26467-X $1.00

A BOY'S WILL AND NORTH OF BOSTON, Robert Frost. 112pp. (Available in U.S. only) 26866-7 $1.00

THE ROAD NOT TAKEN AND OTHER POEMS, Robert Frost. 64pp. (Available in U.S. only) 27550-7 $1.00

A SHROPSHIRE LAD, A. E. Housman. 64pp. 26468-8 $1.00

"LORD RANDAL" AND OTHER BRITISH BALLADS, Francis James Child (ed.). 64pp. 28987-7 $1.00

"TO HIS COY MISTRESS" AND OTHER POEMS, Andrew Marvell. 64pp. 29544-3 $1.00

LYRIC POEMS, John Keats. 80pp. 26871-3 $1.00

THE BOOK OF PSALMS, King James Bible. 128pp. 27541-8 $1.50

GUNGA DIN AND OTHER FAVORITE POEMS, Rudyard Kipling. 80pp. 26471-8 $1.00

THE CONGO AND OTHER POEMS, Vachel Lindsay. 96pp. 27272-9 $1.00

FAVORITE POEMS, Henry Wadsworth Longfellow. 96pp. 27273-7 $1.00

SPOON RIVER ANTHOLOGY, Edgar Lee Masters. 144pp. 27275-3 $1.50

DOVER · THRIFT · EDITIONS

POETRY

"MINIVER CHEEVY" AND OTHER POEMS, Edwin Arlington Robinson. 64pp. 28756-4 $1.00

EARLY POEMS, Ezra Pound. 80pp. (Available in U.S. only) 28745-9 $1.00

EARLY POEMS, William Carlos Williams. 64pp. (Available in U.S. only) 29294-0 $1.00

"THE WASTE LAND" AND OTHER POEMS, T. S. Eliot. 64pp. (Available in U.S. only) 40061-1 $1.00

RENASCENCE AND OTHER POEMS, Edna St. Vincent Millay. 64pp. (Available in U.S. only) 26873-X $1.00

SELECTED POEMS, John Milton. 128pp. 27554-X $1.50

SELECTED CANTERBURY TALES, Geoffrey Chaucer. 144pp. 28241-4 $1.00

GREAT SONNETS, Paul Negri (ed.). 96pp. 28052-7 $1.00

CIVIL WAR POETRY: An Anthology, Paul Negri. 128pp. 29883-3 $1.50

WAR IS KIND AND OTHER POEMS, Stephen Crane. 64pp. 40424-2 $1.00

THE RAVEN AND OTHER FAVORITE POEMS, Edgar Allan Poe. 64pp. 26685-0 $1.00

ESSAY ON MAN AND OTHER POEMS, Alexander Pope. 128pp. 28053-5 $1.50

GOBLIN MARKET AND OTHER POEMS, Christina Rossetti. 64pp. 28055-1 $1.00

CHICAGO POEMS, Carl Sandburg. 80pp. 28057-8 $1.00

THE SHOOTING OF DAN MCGREW AND OTHER POEMS, Robert Service. 96pp. (Available in U.S. only) 27556-6 $1.00

COMPLETE SONNETS, William Shakespeare. 80pp. 26686-9 $1.00

SELECTED POEMS, Percy Bysshe Shelley. 128pp. 27558-2 $1.50

100 BEST-LOVED POEMS, Philip Smith (ed.). 96pp. 28553-7 $1.00

101 GREAT AMERICAN POEMS, The American Poetry & Literacy Project (ed.). (Available in U.S. only) 40158-8 $1.00

NATIVE AMERICAN SONGS AND POEMS: An Anthology, Brian Swann (ed.). 64pp. 29450-1 $1.00

SELECTED POEMS, Alfred Lord Tennyson. 112pp. 27282-6 $1.00

LITTLE ORPHANT ANNIE AND OTHER POEMS, James Whitcomb Riley. 80pp. 28260-0 $1.00

CHRISTMAS CAROLS: COMPLETE VERSES, Shane Weller (ed.). 64pp. 27397-0 $1.00

GREAT LOVE POEMS, Shane Weller (ed.). 128pp. 27284-2 $1.00

LOVE: A Book of Quotations, Herb Galewitz (ed.). 64pp. 40004-2 $1.00

EVANGELINE AND OTHER POEMS, Henry Wadsworth Longfellow. 64pp. 28255-4 $1.00

CIVIL WAR POETRY AND PROSE, Walt Whitman. 96pp. 28507-3 $1.00

SELECTED POEMS, Walt Whitman. 128pp. 26878-0 $1.00

THE BALLAD OF READING GAOL AND OTHER POEMS, Oscar Wilde. 64pp. 27072-6 $1.00

FAVORITE POEMS, William Wordsworth. 80pp. 27073-4 $1.00

WORLD WAR ONE BRITISH POETS: Brooke, Owen, Sassoon, Rosenberg and Others, Candace Ward (ed.). (Available in U.S. only) 29568-0 $1.00

THE CAVALIER POETS: An Anthology, Thomas Crofts (ed.). 80pp. 28766-1 $1.00

ENGLISH ROMANTIC POETRY: An Anthology, Stanley Appelbaum (ed.). 256pp. 29282-7 $2.00

EARLY POEMS, William Butler Yeats. 128pp. 27808-5 $1.50

"EASTER, 1916" AND OTHER POEMS, William Butler Yeats. 80pp. (Available in U.S. only) 29771-3 $1.00

DOVER·THRIFT·EDITIONS

FICTION

FLATLAND: A ROMANCE OF MANY DIMENSIONS, Edwin A. Abbott. 96pp. 27263-X $1.00

PERSUASION, Jane Austen. 224pp. 29555-9 $2.00

PRIDE AND PREJUDICE, Jane Austen. 272pp. 28473-5 $2.00

SENSE AND SENSIBILITY, Jane Austen. 272pp. 29049-2 $2.00

WUTHERING HEIGHTS, Emily Brontë. 256pp. 29256-8 $2.00

BEOWULF, Beowulf (trans. by R. K. Gordon). 64pp. 27264-8 $1.00

CIVIL WAR STORIES, Ambrose Bierce. 128pp. 28038-1 $1.00

THE AUTOBIOGRAPHY OF AN EX-COLORED MAN, James Weldon Johnson. 112pp. 28512-X $1.00

TARZAN OF THE APES, Edgar Rice Burroughs. 224pp. (Available in U.S. only) 29570-2 $2.00

ALICE'S ADVENTURES IN WONDERLAND, Lewis Carroll. 96pp. 27543-4 $1.00

O PIONEERS!, Willa Cather. 128pp. 27785-2 $1.00

MY ÁNTONIA, Willa Cather. 176pp. 28240-6 $2.00

PAUL'S CASE AND OTHER STORIES, Willa Cather. 64pp. 29057-3 $1.00

IN A GERMAN PENSION: 13 Stories, Katherine Mansfield. 112pp. 28719-X $1.50

THE STORY OF AN AFRICAN FARM, Olive Schreiner. 256pp. 40165-0 $2.00

"THE YELLOW WALLPAPER" AND OTHER STORIES, Charlotte Perkins Gilman. 80pp. 29857-4 $1.00

HERLAND, Charlotte Perkins Gilman. 128pp. 40429-3 $1.50

FIVE GREAT SHORT STORIES, Anton Chekhov. 96pp. 26463-7 $1.00

"THE FIDDLER OF THE REELS" AND OTHER SHORT STORIES, Thomas Hardy. 80pp. 29960-0 $1.50

FAVORITE FATHER BROWN STORIES, G. K. Chesterton. 96pp. 27545-0 $1.00

THE WARDEN, Anthony Trollope. 176pp. 40076-X $2.00

THE COUNTRY OF THE POINTED FIRS, Sarah Orne Jewett. 96pp. 28196-5 $1.00

GREAT SHORT STORIES BY AMERICAN WOMEN, Candace Ward (ed.). 192pp. 28776-9 $2.00

SHORT STORIES, Louisa May Alcott. 64pp. 29063-8 $1.00

THE AWAKENING, Kate Chopin. 128pp. 27786-0 $1.00

A PAIR OF SILK STOCKINGS AND OTHER STORIES, Kate Chopin. 64pp. 29264-9 $1.00

THE REVOLT OF "MOTHER" AND OTHER STORIES, Mary E. Wilkins Freeman. 128pp. 40428-5 $1.50

HEART OF DARKNESS, Joseph Conrad. 80pp. 26464-5 $1.00

THE SECRET SHARER AND OTHER STORIES, Joseph Conrad. 128pp. 27546-9 $1.00

THE "LITTLE REGIMENT" AND OTHER CIVIL WAR STORIES, Stephen Crane. 80pp. 29557-5 $1.00

THE OPEN BOAT AND OTHER STORIES, Stephen Crane. 128pp. 27547-7 $1.50

THE RED BADGE OF COURAGE, Stephen Crane. 112pp. 26465-3 $1.00

A CHRISTMAS CAROL, Charles Dickens. 80pp. 26865-9 $1.00

THE CRICKET ON THE HEARTH AND OTHER CHRISTMAS STORIES, Charles Dickens. 128pp. 28039-X $1.00

THE DOUBLE, Fyodor Dostoyevsky. 128pp. 29572-9 $1.50

NOTES FROM THE UNDERGROUND, Fyodor Dostoyevsky. 96pp. 27053-X $1.00

THE GAMBLER, Fyodor Dostoyevsky. 112pp. 29081-6 $1.50

THE ADVENTURE OF THE DANCING MEN AND OTHER STORIES, Sir Arthur Conan Doyle. 80pp. 29558-3 $1.00

THE HOUND OF THE BASKERVILLES, Arthur Conan Doyle. 128pp. 28214-7 $1.00

SIX GREAT SHERLOCK HOLMES STORIES, Sir Arthur Conan Doyle. 112pp. 27055-6 $1.00

SILAS MARNER, George Eliot. 160pp. 29246-0 $1.50

DOVER · THRIFT · EDITIONS

FICTION

MADAME BOVARY, Gustave Flaubert. 256pp. 29257-6 $2.00

WHERE ANGELS FEAR TO TREAD, E. M. Forster. 128pp. (Available in U.S. only) 27791-7 $1.50

A ROOM WITH A VIEW, E. M. Forster. 176pp. (Available in U.S. only) 28467-0 $2.00

THE OVERCOAT AND OTHER STORIES, Nikolai Gogol. 112pp. 27057-2 $1.50

GREAT GHOST STORIES, John Grafton (ed.). 112pp. 27270-2 $1.00

"THE MOONLIT ROAD" AND OTHER GHOST AND HORROR STORIES, Ambrose Bierce (John Grafton, ed.) 96pp. 40056-5 $1.00

THE MABINOGION, Lady Charlotte E. Guest. 192pp. 29541-9 $2.00

WINESBURG, OHIO, Sherwood Anderson. 160pp. 28269-4 $2.00

THE LUCK OF ROARING CAMP AND OTHER STORIES, Bret Harte. 96pp. 27271-0 $1.00

THIS SIDE OF PARADISE, F. Scott Fitzgerald. 208pp. 28999-0 $2.00

"THE DIAMOND AS BIG AS THE RITZ" AND OTHER STORIES, F. Scott Fitzgerald. 29991-0 $2.00

THE SCARLET LETTER, Nathaniel Hawthorne. 192pp. 28048-9 $2.00

YOUNG GOODMAN BROWN AND OTHER STORIES, Nathaniel Hawthorne. 128pp. 27060-2 $1.00

THE GIFT OF THE MAGI AND OTHER SHORT STORIES, O. Henry. 96pp. 27061-0 $1.00

THE NUTCRACKER AND THE GOLDEN POT, E. T. A. Hoffmann. 128pp. 27806-9 $1.00

THE BEAST IN THE JUNGLE AND OTHER STORIES, Henry James. 128pp. 27552-3 $1.00

DAISY MILLER, Henry James. 64pp. 28773-4 $1.00

WASHINGTON SQUARE, Henry James. 176pp. 40431-5 $2.00

THE TURN OF THE SCREW, Henry James. 96pp. 26684-2 $1.00

DUBLINERS, James Joyce. 160pp. 26870-5 $1.00

A PORTRAIT OF THE ARTIST AS A YOUNG MAN, James Joyce. 192pp. 28050-0 $2.00

DEATH IN VENICE, Thomas Mann. 96pp. (Available in U.S. only) 28714-9 $1.00

THE METAMORPHOSIS AND OTHER STORIES, Franz Kafka. 96pp. 29030-1 $1.50

THE MAN WHO WOULD BE KING AND OTHER STORIES, Rudyard Kipling. 128pp. 28051-9 $1.50

SREDNI VASHTAR AND OTHER STORIES, Saki (H. H. Munro). 96pp. 28521-9 $1.00

THE OIL JAR AND OTHER STORIES, Luigi Pirandello. 96pp. 28459-X $1.00

SELECTED SHORT STORIES, D. H. Lawrence. 128pp. 27794-1 $1.00

GREEN TEA AND OTHER GHOST STORIES, J. Sheridan LeFanu. 96pp. 27795-X $1.00

SHORT STORIES, Theodore Dreiser. 112pp. 28215-5 $1.50

THE CALL OF THE WILD, Jack London. 64pp. 26472-6 $1.00

FIVE GREAT SHORT STORIES, Jack London. 96pp. 27063-7 $1.00

WHITE FANG, Jack London. 160pp. 26968-X $1.00

THE NECKLACE AND OTHER SHORT STORIES, Guy de Maupassant. 128pp. 27064-5 $1.00

BARTLEBY AND BENITO CERENO, Herman Melville. 112pp. 26473-4 $1.00

THE GOLD-BUG AND OTHER TALES, Edgar Allan Poe. 128pp. 26875-6 $1.00

TALES OF TERROR AND DETECTION, Edgar Allan Poe. 96pp. 28744-0 $1.00

DETECTION BY GASLIGHT, Douglas G. Greene (ed.). 272pp. 29928-7 $2.00

THE THIRTY-NINE STEPS, John Buchan. 96pp. 28201-5 $1.50

THE QUEEN OF SPADES AND OTHER STORIES, Alexander Pushkin. 128pp. 28054-3 $1.50

FIRST LOVE AND DIARY OF A SUPERFLUOUS MAN, Ivan Turgenev. 96pp. 28775-0 $1.50

FATHERS AND SONS, Ivan Turgenev. 176pp. 40073-5 $2.00

FRANKENSTEIN, Mary Shelley. 176pp. 28211-2 $1.00

THREE LIVES, Gertrude Stein. 176pp. (Available in U.S. only) 28059-4 $2.00

DOVER · THRIFT · EDITIONS

FICTION

THE STRANGE CASE OF DR. JEKYLL AND MR. HYDE, Robert Louis Stevenson. 64pp. 26688-5 $1.00

TREASURE ISLAND, Robert Louis Stevenson. 160pp. 27559-0 $1.50

THE LOST WORLD, Arthur Conan Doyle. 176pp. 40060-3 $1.50

GULLIVER'S TRAVELS, Jonathan Swift. 240pp. 29273-8 $2.00

ROBINSON CRUSOE, Daniel Defoe. 288pp. 40427-7 $2.00

THE KREUTZER SONATA AND OTHER SHORT STORIES, Leo Tolstoy. 144pp. 27805-0 $1.50

THE IMMORALIST, André Gide. 112pp. (Available in U.S. only) 29237-1 $1.50

ADVENTURES OF HUCKLEBERRY FINN, Mark Twain. 224pp. 28061-6 $2.00

THE ADVENTURES OF TOM SAWYER, Mark Twain. 192pp. 40077-8 $2.00

THE MYSTERIOUS STRANGER AND OTHER STORIES, Mark Twain. 128pp. 27069-6 $1.00

HUMOROUS STORIES AND SKETCHES, Mark Twain. 80pp. 29279-7 $1.00

YOU KNOW ME AL, Ring Lardner. 128pp. 28513-8 $1.00

MOLL FLANDERS, Daniel Defoe. 256pp. 29093-X $2.00

CANDIDE, Voltaire (François-Marie Arouet). 112pp. 26689-3 $1.00

"THE COUNTRY OF THE BLIND" AND OTHER SCIENCE-FICTION STORIES, H. G. Wells. 160pp. (Available in U.S. only) 29569-9 $1.00

THE ISLAND OF DR. MOREAU, H. G. Wells. (Available in U.S. only) 29027-1 $1.00

THE INVISIBLE MAN, H. G. Wells. 112pp. (Available in U.S. only) 27071-8 $1.00

THE TIME MACHINE, H. G. Wells. 80pp. (Available in U.S. only) 28472-7 $1.00

LOOKING BACKWARD, Edward Bellamy. 160pp. 29038-7 $2.00

THE WAR OF THE WORLDS, H. G. Wells. 160pp. (Available in U.S. only) 29506-0 $1.00

ETHAN FROME, Edith Wharton. 96pp. 26690-7 $1.00

SHORT STORIES, Edith Wharton. 128pp. 28235-X $1.00

THE AGE OF INNOCENCE, Edith Wharton. 288pp. 29803-5 $2.00

THE MOON AND SIXPENCE, W. Somerset Maugham. 176pp. (Available in U.S. only) 28731-9 $2.00

THE PICTURE OF DORIAN GRAY, Oscar Wilde. 192pp. 27807-7 $1.50

MONDAY OR TUESDAY: Eight Stories, Virginia Woolf. 64pp. (Available in U.S. only) 29453-6 $1.00

JACOB'S ROOM, Virginia Woolf. 144pp. (Available in U.S. only) 40109-X $1.50

NONFICTION

THE DEVIL'S DICTIONARY, Ambrose Bierce. 144pp. 27542-6 $1.00

DE PROFUNDIS, Oscar Wilde. 64pp. 29308-4 $1.00

OSCAR WILDE'S WIT AND WISDOM: A Book of Quotations, Oscar Wilde. 64pp. 40146-4 $1.00

THE SOULS OF BLACK FOLK, W. E. B. Du Bois. 176pp. 28041-1 $2.00

NARRATIVE OF THE LIFE OF FREDERICK DOUGLASS, Frederick Douglass. 96pp. 28499-9 $1.00

NARRATIVE OF SOJOURNER TRUTH, Sojourner Truth. 80pp. 29899-X $1.00

UP FROM SLAVERY, Booker T. Washington. 160pp. 28738-6 $2.00

A VINDICATION OF THE RIGHTS OF WOMAN, Mary Wollstonecraft. 224pp. 29036-0 $2.00

THE SUBJECTION OF WOMEN, John Stuart Mill. 112pp. 29601-6 $1.50

TAO TE CHING, Lao Tze. 112pp. 29792-6 $1.00

THE ANALECTS, Confucius. 128pp. 28484-0 $2.00

SELF-RELIANCE AND OTHER ESSAYS, Ralph Waldo Emerson. 128pp. 27790-9 $1.00

SELECTED ESSAYS, Michel de Montaigne. 96pp. 29109-X $1.50